How to Hang the Moon

Poems by Huascar Medina

Kansas City Spartan Press Missouri

Spartan Press
Kansas City, Missouri
spartanpresskc.com

Spartan
Press

This book was originally published as part of the Spartan Press
POP Poetry Series, which ran from 2015 to 2017.

Radio and *Surrogate City* were published in Reverberated Echoes:
A Kansas City Reader by Asinimali Press.
Per Aspera Ad Astra was featured on an online zine 150kansaspoems.
wordpress.com.

TABLE OF CONTENTS

To Cal,
For pulling stones out of my pockets.

Spanish Knotted Feather Stitching

Only Neruda can save us
I've written him a plea for guidance
addressed it to the waning crystal moon
on that red branch of the now gone
autumn in his window

Its cinched with thread to a paloma
whom refused to wear the satchel
my Aquellita knitted through manos anudado
before her passing

El paloma argued for practicality,
balance and against my need for sentimentality
The added weight of things
makes flight onerous he'd say

How I wish this bird was more passenger pigeon
…less dove

Willing to fight through wind and rain to get there
Okay with war and loss

I even taught him to fly in cursive
In case he didn't make it
Before he's shot down
So others may see
the phrases passing by
But very few people see the need for
soft…round…words
free and flowing in the air

His grace appeared indecisive
Almost lost from below
How they've pitied him
Poor paloma

I beg of you
Please
Takes this note to his shores
Sing towards the sill in his view
Be candid

Have manners
Wipe the sand from your feet before entering
Bathe in his café
Perch yourself upon his finger piece

I just have to know
Can a song of despair come before a love poem?

The Obituary Writer

I want to write poems for poets;
the kind that don't get published.
Whispers in a secret tongue only you
can understand. I want you to
love the way I love words; as if
you're the only living thing; as if
you were reading your spouse's obituary.
The one that only you could write; that
everyone else can feel, but
barely understand.

This is for you.

Under the Streetlamps

During summer evenings
I watch the starlings perched on power lines
        Waiting for a season

You could walk with me you know
Hand in hand
        Before the fall
Like this sidewalk cliff summits above everything
And I'm all you can hold onto

Don't let go
We won't be judged
I promise
They'll probably sing the songs of car alarms

Warn us
That things locked up can still be

stolen

Wading in the Pool

Synchronous worry
Barely afloat
You swam collegiately
Division 2
Got a scholarship
Got a degree
Got a desk
Got two monitors
Got laid off

Vacating the patio you remember
Why you went out there
—To escape the home
Walls painted mortgage
Whatever color that is
That's the color of these walls
An off-white with no gloss
Eggshell cracking

Entering
You don't even dry yourself off
Footprints evaporate
A wraith abandoned

You remind yourself
Sandals are for beaches, locker rooms
and prisons; real prisons
not ones with diving boards

Bastard

Adam's mother never approved of Lilith
She couldn't fathom they were raised
from this earth as equals.

It was a reminder that she was
not loved by her man; not good enough.
He had left her with child in Eden;
the zoo with no cages.

Adam my poor boy…
you've lied to creation;
to lay with Eve

Your own mother…Adam,
the giver of your life…Adam;
just so you may have your way.
Adam…
your guilt erases her from memory.
What was her name?

Adam…

What have you done?

Adam…

your father has left.

Adam…

it was not her fault.

Adam…

are you even listening?

Adam…

Adam…

Adam…

Saul Williams Was Right

I will never understand why we refer to God
as himself?

                                   God is a she.

Creation is birth
and man has no womb.

Did he spit us out,
    shit us out,
        or piss us out?

None of the above,
there is no dignity in that narrative.

God is a she.
Creation is birth.

Bad Poet

I never wanted to write a poem about cicadas.

Much less, have it published.

I don't want to *Milk the game*

or con some editor into believing

I was there.

But tonight I want to write,

in peace and quiet,

without those god-damn cicadas,

loud in everything I do.

Surrogate City

Mama, *Estoy Bien.*

Mother KC has adopted me.
She too wears ironed garments
of concrete and glass,
winks at me to cross the streets,
reminds me I am cared for
through sirens in the air.

She hums a highway lullaby
of old Paseo Puente;
so I may pass the nights,
skylines don't resemble
mi vieja san ciudad in peace.

She embraces
your son
the sun
el sol
my soul.

KC has been good to me.

Don't Marry Giants

…that big, dark, hunky boy, the only one there huge enough for me.
-Sylvia Plath's diary entry February 26, 1956
a day after meeting Ted Hughes.

I want to build a time machine and go back
to when women were ladies and dresses were casual.
When only husbands could be gentlemen
and a ring-less finger was a prick.
I would move to Devon and become a gardener.
I would have an affair with Sylvia and purposely get caught.
Muddy boot prints would lead him to a shaky bedside where
he would find us with Jazz, Wordsworth and daffodils;
naked,
sweaty and whispering poetry
into each other's mouths.
I hope it hurts him.

Then she could divorce him
prior to his complete consumption of every piece

of precut paper thinly sliced confession.
I'd leave her an anthology of love letters as goodbye,
jump into my time machine and return to today somber.

It would be worth it though,
so I could read her poetry about me,
in *The New Yorker,*
in the not too distant past;
aptly titled,
That Little Prick.

Virginia Woolf and the Instrument
of My Desire

I imagine you,
in the privacy of your room,
bone in hand,
before the vanity
with daylight guiding

You thought of me,
how I've always whispered flirtations
in your ear while we sat stranded
amongst strangers pretending to be proper

You are so considerate love,
to wear your hair that way;
allowing me a glimpse of
where the words you conjure ideate.

Hollywood Kisses

I wish our lips were made of Tungsten.
I'd name one Ali and your other MacGraw.
They'd meet mine Ryan and O'neal and
we'd shoot a love story with no direction,
use a Bell & Howell 8mm camera with no film;
so we wouldn't have to cut.

It'll sound like tap dancing
to the passerby wondering why
and what rhythms we are hearing
in the scores of our hearts;
as we close our eyes
and keep the Jazz inside.

Fin

I would have been your Robert Taylor
if you had an ounce of Greta Garbo
in your bones.

You see,
these words can be as black and white
as any motion picture;
romance or tragedy.

How to Start a Fire

You begin by gathering
every inflammable fiber
you can muster.

Take a deep breath,
calm your fear of burning away;
then accept that all that may be left
are ashes if we fail.

Not all fires can be contained,
some never ignite;
no matter how much friction
you create or kindle.

Go forth now,
find a quite secluded place,
away from all the elements
we can never control,
grab him by the hand,
look him in the eyes and say,
I love you.

Coal Ash

We kissed so deep
our spirits gave birth to
children who held hands as we slept.
They sang folksongs as they
danced around our tickers;
like a flower on fire.

What a beautiful thing to burn
— this our Great Plague,
the blazing of our bodies,
ashes gathering in the center
of our irises.

Dear Love,

I will always love you. I will always love you. I will always love
you. I will always love you. I will always love you. I will always
love you. I will always love you. I will always love you. I will
always love you. I will always love you. I will always love you.
I will always love you. I will always love you. I will always love
you. I will always love you. I will always love you. I will always
love you. I will always love you. I will always love you. I will
always love you. I will always love you. I will always love you.
I will always love you. I will always love you. I will always love
you. I will always love you. I will always love you. I will always
love you. I will always love you. I will always love you. I will
always love you. I will always love you.

Love,
Me

Saboteur's Ode

I will follow you
hand in hand
into the shade
cast by
giant statues of morality

We will hand make
beaded charm bracelets of dynamite
mime our intent
in a two person powwow
underneath a canopy of darkness
with holes poked in it
where we find our spirit animals
dancing
like ancient constellations
under the flaming lights

— wildfires
started by rubbing our lips
into smoke and ash

as we tickle the heat
with taller-than-us fuses
marionettes of destruction
yearning in a dangling hunger
for ignition.

Once lit
we will hold each other
under the tiny stars of anticipation
the fire flies of warning
in the fields of our hopelessness
at the bottom
of the edifice of mores
waiting to explode into
tiny embers of
Godliness.

The crowds of strangers will
try to put us out
with buckets full of reason
and dissent
wondering why
heated imprints

of a fox and spider
entangled
survived unscathed
in a
patch of grass
amongst
the black burnt earth
of creation

long after
the slash and burn
of desire
scorched the village
and left the townsfolk
surrounded by remnants of idolatry
nowhere to run
and the taste of hallelujahs
on their tongues

Il n'y a pas de temps pour l'amour dans sa vie.

Maybe in death,
if the end drew near,
I'd soak the hotel mattress in moonshine,
fill the room with dollar store candles,
bathe in Champagne and then leave the towel off;
with Mahler's Symphony No' 9
dolente in the distance,
waiting for a flame to ignite; so
we may die in each other's arms,
without all that Shakespeare fucking up
a good love poem about
Chinaski being left behind,
playing God
with fancy man made rapture.

Circus

Bury me at Showmen's Rest.
I, too, am a train wreck.

A daredevil, walking tightropes
tied to no edges; iron rod in hand.
A strongman, taming lions caged;
swallowing these words.

I am the clown,
covered in his laughter
after burning left her marked,
Female Unidentified
and I a roustabout.
I am in the Gaslight
putting on a show,
everyone is cheering,
so I drink my Kerosene
late into the night.

Bury me at Showmen's Rest.
I, too, am a train wreck.

Sounds of Self-Destruction

Speakers too close to hearts
can be unpleasant; infinite loops
in self-destruction. We avoided feedback and
distorted songs of, *I love you.* We should've been
silence.

Silence too close to hearts
can be unpleasant; infinite loops
in self-destruction. We avoided feedback and
distorted songs of, *I love you.* We should've been
speakers

Speakers too close to hearts
can be unpleasant; infinite loops
in self-destruction. We avoided feedback and
distorted songs of, *I love you.* We should've been
silence.

Silence too close to hearts
can be unpleasant; infinite loops
in self-destruction. We avoided feedback and
distorted songs of, *I love you*. We should've been
speakers.

Speakers too close to hearts
can be unpleasant; infinite loops
in self-destruction. We avoided feedback and
distorted songs of, *I love you.* We should've been
silence.

Radio

I'm afraid of Jazz after midnight,
when all the liquid fills my spirit,
when the time to head home comes
too soon.

I'm afraid I'll keep driving,
lured by the city in the radio;
the siren in the horn.

As I flirt with floating stage lights,
intersecting with other ways to
lose myself.

I want to be where the music's at,
ahead of me in some distant juke box,
on a tiny stage; twice the size of a bar top.

Where country boys go to be
city legends; not remembered
but thought of often.

The Seductress by Wynton Marsalis

When I hear him,
I let go of false notions of Class, Classics and Classical.
I dissipate. I'm a songstress with ink for voice.
I break the bars, measures and refrains lived in. I feel
the sounds of notes bent on the end like secret maps to
harmony.

Emotions echoed this hard are songs in rhythm
with amplified hearts tied to down beats. I want
a soul of Jazz; to fly with the music. I need to
breathe in heaven and exhale hell; so I can
feel the white and black of this sheet with
the hands of Monk and delve into the space between.
— Find those notes that we would have missed if we
only cared
for Class, Classics and Classical.

I want to be that Jazz.
I need to feel his hand on the tip of that horn;

grasping as if his life depended on it,
muting just enough to keep Gabriel at bay,
as if another note played would be too much,
that if he played again he would lose his love for it
and be less trumpet; nothing more than tinkling brass.

Fatherland

I wish I didn't feel like your father,
that we were more brother;
so we could rebel this life of youth and age
together.

We would be copilots over the Pacific Ocean,
running out of fuel at the point of no return.
We would fight a war with F bombs
in the name of our Motherland.

We'd play music too loud
to understand what the other was saying.
We would ride with the windows down,
turn the volume up and yell louder.

In those moments,
we would share secrets about our enemies
how much we resemble our fathers; then
we would sit silently and motionless

… return home a little less defeated than before.

His Nature

There are days these words find me,
crawling down my tongue at leisure;
the stroll of ants on leaves, but
there are other days I hum insistent;
that every word be freed. My mouth
a hornets nest knocked out of a tree.

On Cats

I've read cats sleep 20 hours a day.
I thought of my cat and how much time I spend
waking him as I come and go as I please.
Waking him from his real life,
somewhere else; faraway from here.

A place where he can be left alone.
Where he doesn't have to beg for
more food,
more attention,
more affection,
more peace,
more quiet,

A place much better than here.

I think of the strays on my street
and their spindled bones;
empty bird cages sagging in their drapery.

I see the key holes they peer through
in the shadows of the alley;
how they suffer in silence.
This is why they tremble in our company.
Shook to the core at the presence of goodness;
fearful of its fleeting nature.
I want to warn them.

Go back!
Go back!
Go BACK to sleep!

This is not for real!
This is not your life!

But I have never done so,
because I am afraid of waking
the homeless man they live with.

Hatchery

You were warned
no one has lived here in years,
but you were eager to abandon caution
like mother without child.

We removed the nature from the lawn,
mowed and trimmed the hedges for hours.
The wood bees fought back,
the lizards hid in the basement
and that Robin sat perched
on the edge of insanity
as you brushed her home out
of our porch with a secondhand
storeroom broom.

The Robin blue eggs were ripe.
Slowly living red flesh seeped out
between the cracks
onto the dusty gray slab of
indifference.

When they tumbled,
I was 10 again full of shame;
I never meant to hurt those birds.
A toy is a weapon for a boy and
a weapon is a toy for a man.

Mother Robin watched us
rake away life like leaves
in autumn until sundown.
I'll never read
Phillip Larkin's *Lawn Mower*
without the guilt
he tried to escape
that day in the yard.

Selene

She covers herself in stars
with the comfort of night.
Laying down devoid
of all colors brushed in light.

She can rest here,
away from day and expectation,
naked, unafraid,
natural and powerful.

Exposing herself at will,
only as she sees fit;
elegant and patient
as *La Luna.*

The Diary of Helios

I prefer those with moonlight,
effortlessly glowing,
softly beaming,
full of afterlight; sharing
the luster of lost loves.

Those who know touch and speak body,
burnished by a rousing fire; reflecting
the warmth of something greater
in the distance.

You are brighter than you've been told,
more beautiful than all the stars combined;
graceful in all your phases;
the only thing worth gazing upon.

You deserve the sky and oceans
as your vanity.

You are still ethereal,
a heavenly body once worshipped;
pure radiance removed from celestial being.

Before time,
before day,
before night,
before the birth of stars
there was us.

Selene,
we were closer then,
almost inseparable.

...try to remember.

Stargazers

I think it's magic,
how tiny lilies
bloom out of your irises;
as light flashes into the dark
wells of your view.
I wonder,
how long they've laid there
dormant;
waiting for the right
air to breathe.
Your eyelashes,
brushing away the skyline;
creating a bit more room
for heaven to
accept us.
Even the sun is in awe,
she sleeps so she may
wake beside you
— one eye open.

Her chagrin,
looming in the moon,
hiding away nightly;
watching every star.
They too are suns
who wish to be closer.

Per Aspera Ad Astra

We were lost in the plains,
beautiful and ordinary,
Sunflowers in the fields;
seeds of fallen stars,
standing tall; deeply rooted
in this land.

I've admired how our flowers shine,
grasping towards the sky
beyond the prairie grass; anchored
down to earth; mimicking
the sun.

When a gardener plants
the seeds of Helianthus, he is
performing magic; raising
stars out of the dust where
buzzing planets circle,

half red moons set; and swarming
comets float in orange comas.

I've always felt that
late at night, in the bed of a truck,
in a Kansas field; we were
at the center of this universe.

...and I was exactly where I should be,
amongst the flowers; not below.

Exposure

She was upset.
Her hands Junipers
beneath the dark wisps of hair
still lighter than the mood,
I stepped away.
No one paints landscapes in black

She became angry.
I've never sketched sadness,
It would be
a single line drawn;
a hyphen that went too far
off the page.

She begged for a photo.
My Holga choked with film,
black and white
hung from a door since winter.

I don't have any color left
She was fine. I was Ansel,
manumitting flickers of light;
capturing the clashes
between heaven and earth,
creating frontlines sundering
love sacred and profane
— *chiaroscuro.*

I developed alone,
two rolls wasted,
empty-titled pics,
red-filtered and soulless.

She was satisfied.
I was not.

There was no creation,
no art that night; just a
break before destruction
a flash of light.

My Siren

She laid within that porcelain shell
pale and unafraid. Her fin
removed in secret to hide
the mystery of her life.
They drained that salt-less ocean
from the tiny mausoleum.
Water distilled by machine and chemical,
made civil; even drinkable to some.

It looked as if she had swept ashore;
drug onto land by loss of tide.
Mother moon didn't want her.
She was a stranger on this land,
a wasted beauty, astray
and never home.
She calls me 'til this day,
singing of peace, the sun and sea;
from behind those synthetic palls.
I hear her daily,
Come this way with me...

I Will Be Buried in a Suit of Nebulas

We die a bit daily,
aging the rebuttal of birth.
If I am to leave this earth,
I hope it is at night
in sleep with dream;
so my mind is filled
with heaven as I go.

I want to use ether as embalming fluid,
wrap the universe around me,
so when my casket is opened
and placed at the parlor;
stars will shine in the darkness.

They will hold my funeral
with the light switch off
without candles so we can
change the meaning of wake
and the tradition of mourning;

take the romance out of dying
and back into living.

My tombstone will have no words,
just a constellation
you've never seen before.

Be Wary of a Common Grave

Do not be set on this earth
you of higher multiplicities
go stare into abysses
reflect universes
infinite and isolate
of fixed and unfixed
dimensions.

Drown in the stars
swallow luminescence
hang like the moon above
prove that you can leave this earth
and still exist.

Do not waste your time
staring into man
you'll find only bone
a dark place insistent
you replace moon and glister
with body as cage.

You are impermanence
not born with the envisage
of lying in the ground
share your absolutes
no poet from beyond speaks
without the accretion of eternity.